NOTES

including
- *Introduction*
- *Life of the Author*
- *Background Material*
- *Character Analyses*
- *Significance of Setting*
- *Summaries and Commentaries*
- *Dickens' Philosophy and Style*
- *Questions for Review*

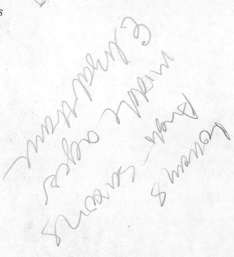

by
Josephine J. Curton, Ph.D.
Department of English
Tallahassee Community College

Cliffs® Notes

INCORPORATED

LINCOLN, NEBRASKA 68501

Editor

Gary Carey, M.A.
University of Colorado

Consulting Editor

James L. Roberts, Ph.D.
Department of English
University of Nebraska

Cliffs Notes, Inc.   Lincoln, Nebraska

INDEX

HARD TIMES

INTRODUCTION

When you read *Hard Times*, you may, at first, decide that its title is inappropriate to the story. The names of the characters, the exaggerated situations, and the satire make for delightful reading; however, it is not a novel for mere entertainment. It is a novel of protest; its voice is that of nineteenth-century English workers.

"Why," you may ask, "should I read a novel concerned with the problems of another era?" The answer is simple: from the literature of the past one learns how better to deal with the present.

These notes are not a substitute for reading *Hard Times;* they are only guides to your understanding of the novel. After all, who would wish to become a member of the school of *FACTS* and deprive himself of the adventure of reading and learning that there is *FANCY* in the world too?

ABOUT THE AUTHOR

The title of Charles Dickens' novel *Hard Times* is an apt designation of his early life and youth. Born February 7, 1812, the boy was one of eight children. His formal education was scanty, but as a child Charles spent much of his time reading and listening to the stories told by his grandmother. His reading included works by Daniel Defoe, Samuel Richardson, Henry Fielding, Oliver Goldsmith, and Tobias Smollett—all outstanding English novelists. Too, young Dickens frequently attended and enjoyed the theater with his uncle.

Charles' father, John Dickens, was a poor manager; consequently, after failing at many jobs, he was arrested and sent to debtor's prison at Marshalsea. All of the family furniture and possessions were sold and Charles went to work in a blackening warehouse. In this job he was treated as a drudge. His mother and family went to Marshalsea; however, Charles, feeling that living in debtors' prison was degrading, did not stay with them, but lived nearby. When the Insolvent Debtors Act resulted in John Dickens' discharge from prison, the family fared better than it had in a long time.

After his father's release, Charles went to school; then he began to work as a clerk for an attorney. Determined to raise his standard of living, he studied shorthand and became a court reporter. Later he began to work for the *Morning Chronicle*. His *Sketches by Boz* (1834-36), which appeared in the *Chronicle,* brought him fame. From this beginning he wrote many books, all of which utilized as characters his own family and people he met. He used for his themes and plots both the working conditions and the social conditions of his time. His Christmas stories, of which *A Christmas Carol* (1843) is most famous, were the only ones which did not describe the plight of his contemporaries. In 1867 he achieved the standard of living which he had set out to attain: he received one hundred thousand dollars for a lecture tour in America. After his return to England in 1870, he died suddenly at the dinner table. Medical men attributed his death to overexertion. Leaving behind a family of four children and a wife to mourn him, Charles Dickens — blackening house apprentice and poor lower middle-class boy — was buried in Westminster Abbey beside other great figures of English literature.

Dickens left behind a large number of much-loved novels, including *Oliver Twist* (1837-39), which satirized the conditions and institutions of the time; *The Old Curiosity Shop* (1840-41), one of the most widely known works in all literature; and *Martin Chuzzlewit* (1843-44), in which Dickens reported his impressions of America. Mrs. Roylance, an early landlady of the author's, appears in *Dombey and Son* (1846-48). *David Copperfield* (1849-50) drew heavily on the writer's own experiences. In *Bleak House* (1852-53) one sees reflected the sorrow that Dickens felt over the deaths of his sister and daughter. In *Hard Times* (1854) he skillfully combined many literary techniques to produce a great novel of social protest. His *Little Dorrit* (1855-57) describes the arrest and imprisonment of his own father. In *A Tale of Two Cities* (1859) a triangle love plot is developed against the background of the French Revolution. *Great Expectations* (1860-61) narrates the growing up of a boy under conditions of mystery and suspense. Dickens' last volume, *Life of Our Lord,* a book for children, was not published until 1934.

In all of his novels — those that appeared as serials in newspapers or magazines and those that were first printed as whole books — Dickens reveals his keen observation, his great understanding of human nature, and his varied techniques of style. True, his characters are sometimes exaggerated; however, the very exaggeration adds vitality and humor to the stories. As a novelist and a social critic, Dickens was a giant of his era; later generations have turned to his works for both amusement and instruction.

BACKGROUND MATERIAL FOR UNDERSTANDING *HARD TIMES*

Since Charles Dickens wrote of the conditions and the people of his time, it is worthwhile to understand the period in which he lived and worked.

No British sovereign since Queen Elizabeth I has exerted such a profound influence on an age as did Queen Victoria (1837-1901). She presided over the period rather than shaped it. The nineteenth century was an age of continual change and unparalleled expansion in almost every field of activity. Not only was it an era of reform, industrialization, achievement in science, government, literature, and world expansion but also a time when man struggled to assert his independence. Man, represented en masse as the laboring class, rose in power and prosperity and gave his voice to government.

There were great intellectual and spiritual disturbances both in society and within the individual. The literature of the period reflects the conflict between the advocates of the triumphant material prosperity of the country and those who felt it had been achieved by the exploitation of human beings at the expense of spiritual and esthetic values. In theory, men of the period committed themselves on the whole to a hard-headed utilitarianism, yet most of the literature is idealistic and romantic.

The prophets of the time deplored the inroads of science upon religious faith; but the Church of England was revivified by the Oxford Movement; evangelical Protestantism was never stronger and more active; and the Roman Catholic Church was becoming an increasingly powerful religious force in England.

Not even in politics were the issues clear-cut. The Whigs prepared the way for the great economic reform of the age, the repeal of the Corn Laws; but it was a Tory leader, Sir Robert Peel, who finally brought that repeal through Parliament.

This century, marked by the Industrial Revolution, was also a century of political and economic unrest in the world: America was torn by the strife of the Civil War; France was faced with the problem of recovery from the wars of Napoleon; and Germany was emerging as a great power.

The Industrial Revolution, though productive of much good, created deplorable living conditions in England. Overcrowding in the cities as a consequence of the population shift from rural to urban areas and the increase in the numbers of immigrants from poverty-stricken Ireland resulted in disease and hunger for thousands of the laboring class. But with the fall of Napoleon, the returning soldiers added not only to the growing numbers of workers but also to the hunger and misery. With the advent of the power loom came unemployment. A surplus labor supply caused wages to drop. Whole families, from the youngest to the oldest, had to enter the factories, the woolen mills, the coal mines, or the cotton mills in order to survive. Children were exploited by employers; for a pittance a day a nine-year-old worked twelve and fourteen hours in the mills, tied to the machines, or in the coal mines pulling carts to take the coal from the shafts. Their fingers were smaller and quicker than those of adults; thus, for picking out the briars and burrs from both cotton and wool, employers preferred to hire children.

Studies of the working and living conditions in England between 1800 and 1834 showed that 82 percent of the workers in the mills were between the ages of eleven and eighteen. Many of these studies proved that 62 percent of the workers in the fabric mills had tuberculosis. The factories were open, barnlike structures, not equipped with any system of heat and ventilation.

These studies, presented to Parliament, resulted in some attempt to bring about reforms in working conditions and to alleviate some of the dire poverty in England. In 1802 the Health Act was passed to provide two hours of instruction for all apprentices. In 1819 a child labor law was enacted which limited to eleven hours a day the working hours of children five to eleven years of age; however, this law was not enforced.

The first great "Victorian" reform antedated Queen Victoria by five years. Until 1832 the old Tudor list of boroughs was still in use. As a result, large towns of recent growth had no representation in Parliament, while some unpopulated localities retained theirs. In essence, the lords who controlled these boroughs (known as rotten boroughs in history) sold seats to the highest bidders. This political pattern was broken when the Reform Bill of 1832 abolished all boroughs with fewer than two thousand inhabitants and decreased by 50 percent the number of representatives admitted from towns with a population between two thousand and four thousand. Only after rioting and a threat of civil war did the House of Lords approve the Reform Bill. With this bill came a new type of Parliament —one with representatives from the rising middle class—and several other important reforms.

In 1833 the Emancipation Bill ended slavery in British colonies, with heavy compensation to the owners. Even though chattel slavery was abolished, industrial slavery continued. Also in 1833 came the first important Factory Law, one which prohibited the employment of children under the age of nine. Under this law children between the ages of nine and thirteen could not work for more than nine hours a day. Night work was prohibited for persons under twenty-one years of age and for all women. By 1849 subsequent legislation provided half day or alternate days of schooling for the factory children, thus cutting down the working hours of children fourteen or under.

The Poor Law of 1834 provided for workhouses; indigent persons, accustomed to living where they pleased, bitterly resented this law, which compelled them to live with their families in workhouses. In fact, the living conditions were so bad that these workhouses were named the "Bastilles of the Poor." Here the poor people, dependent upon the government dole, were subjected to the inhuman treatment of cruel supervisors; an example is Mr. Bumble in Dickens' *Oliver Twist*. If the people rejected this rule of body and soul, they had two alternatives as the machines took more jobs and the wages dropped — either steal or starve. Conditions in prisons were even more deplorable than in the workhouses. Debtors' prison, as revealed in Dickens' *David Copperfield*, was a penalty worse than death.

The undemocratic character of the Reform Bill of 1832, the unpopularity of the Poor Law, and the unhappy conditions of the laborers led to the Chartist Movement of the 1840's. The demands of the Chartist Movement were the abolition of property qualifications for members of Parliament, salaries for members of Parliament, annual election of Parliament, equal electoral districts, equal manhood suffrage, and voting by secret ballot. Chartism, the most formidable working-class movement England had ever seen, failed. The Chartists had no way to identify their cause with the interests of any influential class. Ultimately, though, most of the ends they sought were achieved through free discussion and legislative action.

In 1846 the Prime Minister, Sir Robert Peel, led the repeal of the Corn Laws of 1815. With the repeal of these laws, which were nothing more than protective tariffs in the interest of the landlords and farmers to prevent the importation of cheap foreign grain, came a period of free trade and a rapid increase in manufacture and commerce which gave the working class an opportunity to exist outside the workhouses.

As the country awoke to the degradation of the working classes, industrial reform proceeded gradually but inevitably, in spite of the advocates of laissez-faire and industrial freedom. The political life of the nineteenth century was tied up with its economic theories. The doctrine of laissez-faire (let alone), first projected by Adam

Smith's *Wealth of Nations,* was later elaborated upon by Jeremy Bentham and T. R. Malthus, whose doctrine of Utility was the principle of "the greatest happiness for the greatest number." In other words, this principle meant that the government should allow the economic situation to adjust itself naturally through the laws of supply and demand. With this system, a man at one extreme becomes a millionaire and at the other, a beggar. Thomas Carlyle called this system of economy "the dismal science." Dickens, influenced by Carlyle, castigated it again and again. The Utilitarians, however, helped bring about the repeal of the Corn Laws and to abolish cruel punishment. When Victoria became queen there were four hundred and thirty-eight offenses punishable by death. During her reign, the death penalty was limited to two offenses—murder and treason. With the softening of the penalties and the stressing of prevention and correction came a decrease in crime.

Even though writers of the period protested human degradation under modern industrialism, the main factor in improvement of conditions for labor was not outside sympathy but the initiative taken by the workers themselves. They learned that organized trade unions were more constructive to their welfare than riots and the destruction of machines, which had occurred during the Chartist Movement. Gradually the laboring classes won the right to help themselves. Trade unions were legalized in 1864; two workingmen candidates were elected to Parliament in 1874.

Karl Marx founded the first International Workingmen's Association in London in 1864; three years later he published *Das Kapital,* a book of modern communism. In 1884 the Fabian Society appeared, headed by Beatrice and Sidney Webb, George Bernard Shaw, and other upper middle-class intellectuals. The Fabians believed that socialism would come about gradually without violence.

Once the rights of the workers were recognized, education became of interest to Parliament. In 1870 the Elementary Education Bill provided education for all; in 1891 free common education for all became compulsory. Poet George Meredith and economist and philosopher John Stuart Mill worked for "female emancipation." From this period of change came such women as Florence Nightingale and Frances Powers.

Politics and economics do not make up the whole of a nation's life. In the nineteenth century both religion and science affected the thought and the literature of the period. In 1833, after the Reform Bill of 1832, a group of Oxford men, dissatisfied with the conditions of the Church of England, began the Oxford Movement with the purpose of bringing about in the Church a reformation which would increase spiritual power and emphasize and restore the Catholic doctrine and ritual. Begun by John Keble, the movement carried on its reforms primarily through a series of papers called *Tracts for the Times*. Chief among the reformers was John Henry Newman, a vicar of St. Mary's.

The second half of Queen Victoria's reign was one of prosperity and advancement in science. Inventions such as the steam engine, the telephone, telegraph, and the wireless made communication easier and simpler. Man became curious about and interested in the unknown. New scientific and philosophic research in the fields of geology and biology influenced the religious mind of England. A series of discoveries with respect to man's origin challenged accepted opinions regarding the universe and man's place in it. Sir Charles Lyell's *Principles of Geology* (1830-33) established a continuous history of life on this planet; Sir Frances Galton did pioneer work in the field of heredity; Charles Darwin's *Origin of Species* gave the world the theory of evolution. *The Origin of Species* maintained that all living creatures had developed through infinite differentiations from a single source. This one work had the most profound influence of all secular writings on the thinking of the period. Following its publication there were three schools of thought concerning man's origin: first, Darwin's evidence did not justify his conclusions; therefore, nothing had changed in man's religious beliefs regarding his origin and creation. Second, Darwin's evidence had left no room for God in the universe; therefore, everything had changed and thinking must change. Third, Darwin's theories simply reaffirmed the Biblical concepts; therefore, "evolution is just God's way of doing things."

The conflict between the theologians and the scientists raged not only throughout the remainder of the century but was inevitably reflected in the literature of the period. Poets of the era can be classified through their attitudes toward religion and science. Alfred Tennyson and Robert Browning stand as poets of faith, whereas Matthew Arnold and Arthur Hugh Clough represent the skeptics and the doubters. Later Victorian verse showed less of the conflict than the earlier.

Historians have called Charles Dickens the greatest of the Victorian novelists. His creative genius was surpassed only by that of Shakespeare. Many later novelists were to feel the influence of this writer, whose voice became the trumpet of protest against economic conditions of the age. George Bernard Shaw once said that *Little Dorrit* was as seditious a book as *Das Kapital*. Thus, according to critics, Dickens' *Hard Times* is a relentless indictment of the callous greed of the Victorian industrial society and its misapplied utilitarian philosophy.

CHARACTERIZATION

A. INTRODUCTION

In *Hard Times* Dickens placed villains, heroes, heroines, and bystanders who are representative of his times. Even though many of these characters have names which indicate their personalities or philosophies, they are not caricatures but people endowed with both good and bad human qualities. Shaped by both internal and external forces, they are like Shakespeare's characters—living, breathing beings who love, hate, sin, and repent. True to the class or caste system of nineteenth-century England, Dickens drew them from four groups: the fading aristocracy, the vulgar rising middle class, the downtrodden but struggling labor class, and the itinerant group, represented by the circus people.

B. MAJOR CHARACTERS

1. Representative of the fading aristocracy are Mrs. Sparsit and James Harthouse.

   a. Mrs. Sparsit, a pathetic, but scheming old lady, earns her living by pouring tea and attending to the other housekeeping duties for Mr. Josiah Bounderby, whom she despises. Sparing with words, she is literally a "sitter," first in Bounderby's home and later in his bank. She lends her respectability and culture to his crude, uneducated environment. Resentful of Bounderby and others who do not have the background that she has, she seemingly accepts Bounderby's philosophy of life. In direct discourse with him, she simpers and hedges; when he is not present, she scorns him and spits on his picture. Throughout the novel, Mrs. Sparsit connives and plans for her own advantage. Her role in the first book is one of waiting and watching; in the second book, she continues this role and enlists the aid of Bitzer, an aspirant to the middle class, to bring revenge upon Bounderby; in the last book she serves as informer and is rewarded by losing her position with Bounderby and by being compelled to live with a hated relative, Lady Scadgers.

b. James Harthouse, the second face of the aristocracy, is a young man who comes to Coketown because he is bored with life. He is employed to advance the interests of a political party. When introduced to Louisa, he becomes infatuated with her and seeks to arouse her love. Taking advantage of Bounderby's absences from home, he goes to see Louisa on various pretexts. When Louisa refuses to elope with him, he leaves Coketown for a foreign country. The only hurt he has received is a blow to his ego or vanity.

2. Characters of the middle class take many faces: the wealthy factory owner, the retired merchant who is a champion of facts, the "whelp," and the beautiful Louisa nurtured in facts. Just as the buildings of Coketown are all alike in shape, so are these people alike.

people shaped by their surroundings

a. Josiah Bounderby, the wealthy middle-aged factory owner of Coketown, is a self-made man. Fabricating a story of his childhood, he has built himself a legend of the abandoned waif who has risen from the gutter to his present

typical in MOBC

position. To add to his "self-made" station in life, this blustering, bragging bounder has told the story of his miserable childhood so long and so loud that he believes it himself. The story is simple: he says that after being abandoned by his mother, he was reared by a drunken grandmother, who took his shoes to buy liquor; he relates often and long how he was on his own as a mere child of seven and how he educated himself in the streets. In the final book, when his story is proved false by the appearance of his mother, who had not abandoned him but who had reared and educated him, he is revealed as a fraud who had, in reality, rejected his own mother. With this revelation and other events came his downfall and eventual death.

An opinionated man, he regards the workers in his factories as "Hands," for they are only that—not people to him. The only truth to him is his own version of truth.

In the first book, as a friend of Thomas Gradgrind, he is intent upon having Louisa, Gradgrind's older daughter, for his wife. In the conclusion of book one he succeeds —by taking Gradgrind's son into the bank—in marrying Louisa, who does not love him; for she has never been taught to love or dream, only to learn facts. True to braggart nature, Bounderby expands the story of his miserable rise to wealth by letting everyone know that he has married the daughter of a wealthy, respectable man.

Book two reveals him more fully as the bounder; however, he is a blind bounder—he does not know that his young wife has found a younger man to whom she is attracted. In the final book, when she leaves him and returns home, his ego cannot stand the blow. He does not change, even though almost everyone and everything around him changes.

b. Gradgrind is the father of five children whom he has reared to learn facts and to believe only in statistics. His wife, a semi-invalid, is simple-minded; although she does not understand his philosophy, she tries to do his bidding. As the book progresses, however, he begins to doubt his own teachings. Mr. Thomas Gradgrind represents the Utilitarian philosophy of the nineteenth century.

In the first book he takes into his home a young girl whose father, a circus clown, has abandoned her. He undertakes her education but fails, since she is the product of another environment. In this book he presents Bounderby's suit for marriage to Louisa and is pleased when she recognizes that wealth is important.

In the second book Gradgrind emerges as a father for the first time. He takes Louisa back into his home after she leaves Bounderby. Having lived with the foundling in his home, he has come to recognize that there are emotions such as love and compassion. When his daughter comes to him as a daughter looking for help and sanction, he reacts as a father.

In the last book Gradgrind abandons his philosophy of facts again to help Tom his wayward son to flee from England so that he will not be imprisoned for theft. Gradgrind also vows to clear the name of an accused worker. Here he learns — much to his regret — that Bitzer, one of his former students, has learned his lesson well; Bitzer refuses to help young Tom escape.

c. Tom Gradgrind, the son, is also a face of the middle class. Having been reared never to wonder, never to doubt facts, and never to entertain any vice or fancy, he rebels as a young man when he leaves his father's home, Stone Lodge, to work in Bounderby's bank. He uses Bounderby's affection for Louisa to gain money for gambling and drink. He urges Louisa to marry Bounderby, since it will be to his own benefit if she does.

Freed from the stringent rule of his father, Tom (whom Dickens has Harthouse name "the whelp") becomes a "man about town." He begins to smoke, to drink, and to gamble. When he becomes involved in gambling debts, he looks to Louisa for help. Finally she becomes weary of helping him and denies him further financial aid. Desperate for money to replace what he has taken from the bank funds, Tom stages a robbery and frames Stephen Blackpool. Just as he uses others, so is he used by James Harthouse, who has designs on Louisa.

At the last, Tom shows his complete degeneration of character. When he realizes that exposure is imminent, he runs away. The only redeeming feature of his character is that he truly loves his sister and ultimately regrets that he has brought her heartache. Escaping from England, he lives and dies a lonely life as an exile. In his last illness he writes to his sister asking her forgiveness and love.

d. Louisa Gradgrind Bounderby, a beautiful girl nurtured in the school of facts, reacts and performs in a manner in keeping with her training until she faces a situation for which her education has left her unprepared. A dutiful daughter, she obeys her father in all things — even to contracting a loveless marriage with Bounderby, a man twice her age. The only emotion that fills her barren life is her love for Tom, her younger brother. Still young when she realizes that her father's system of education has failed her, she begins to discover the warmth and compassion of life. Only after her emotional conflict with Harthouse does she start her complete re-education.

3. Dickens employs Biblical parallels to portray the characters of the struggling working class. Stephen Blackpool, an honest, hard-working power-loom weaver in Bounderby's factory and the first victim to the labor cause, is likened unto the Biblical Stephen, the first Christian martyr. Just as the Biblical Stephen was stoned by his own people, so is Stephen Blackpool shunned and despised by his own class. Even though he realizes that Bounderby and the other factory owners are abusing the workers and that something must be done to help them, he refuses to join the union. He

is perceptive enough to know that Slackbridge, the trade-union agitator, is a false prophet to the people.

Married to a woman who had left him years before the story opens, Stephen finds himself hopelessly in love with Rachael, also a worker in the factory. Rachael is likened unto the long-suffering woman of the same name in Biblical history. Stephen cannot marry his beloved because the laws of England are for the rich, not the penniless workman. When he goes to Bounderby for help to obtain a divorce from his drunken, degenerate wife, he is scorned and bullied until he speaks up, denying Bounderby's taunts. On another occasion he defends the workers against Bounderby's scathing remarks; consequently, he is fired and has to seek a job in another town. When Stephen learns that he is accused of theft, he starts back to Coketown to clear his name; however, he does not arrive there. He falls into an abandoned mine pit and is found and rescued minutes before his death. Although he is just one of the "Hands" to Bounderby and others of the middle class, Stephen Blackpool is a very sensitive, religious man who bears no enmity toward those who have hurt him.

4. The last social group that Dickens pictures is best represented by Cecilia "Sissy" Jupe, who is the antithesis of the scholars of Gradgrind's school. This group, the circus people whose endeavor is to make people happy, is scorned by the Gradgrinds and the Bounderbys of the world. Sissy, forsaken by her father, who believed that she would have a better life away from the circus, is a warm, loving individual who brings warmth and understanding to the Gradgrind home. Because of her influence, the younger girl, Jane Gradgrind, grows up to know love, to dream, and to wonder. In the conclusion of the book, Sissy can look forward to a life blessed by a husband and children. The handwriting on the wall foretells her happiness and Louisa's unhappiness.

C. MINOR CHARACTERS
Dickens used the minor characters for comic relief, for transition of plot, and for comparison and contrast.

1. Bitzer is a well-crammed student in Gradgrind's model school of Fact. He is the living contrast to the humble, loving, compassionate Sissy. Bitzer can best be characterized as the symbolic embodiment of the practical Gradgrindian philosophy: he is colorless, servile, mean; and he lives by self-interest.

2. Mr. M'Choakumchild, a teacher in Gradgrind's model school, is an advocate of the Gradgrind system. Dickens says that he might have been a better teacher had he known less.

3. Slackbridge, symbolized as the false prophet to the laboring class, is the trade-union agitator.

4. Mrs. Pegler is the mysterious woman who shows great interest in Mr. Bounderby. One meets her, usually, standing outside the Bounderby house, watching quietly.

5. Adam Smith Gradgrind and Malthus Gradgrind are Thomas Gradgrind's two youngest sons. Their names are in keeping with the economic concern of the book.

6. Members of the Sleary Circus, in addition to Mr. Sleary, are Emma Gordon, Kidderminster, who plays the role of cupid; Mr. E. W. B. Childers, and Josephine Sleary.

7. Unnamed characters are members of the "Hands" and the sick wife of Stephen Blackpool.

SIGNIFICANCE OF SETTING

Settings can be classified as scenic, essential, and symbolic. Scenic is self-explanatory; it is there, but it does not influence the story. Essential means that the story could not have happened any other place or at any other time. A symbolic setting is one which plays an important role in the philosophy of the book. Such a setting is Coketown, England. Coketown, with all its brick buildings and its conformity and sterility and the Educational System, is conspicuous as part of the setting. Dickens uses many symbols to convey the horror of the setting: Coketown is the brick jungle; the factories are the mad elephants; the death-bringing smoke is the serpent; the machinery is the monster. The sameness, the conformity, creates an atmosphere of horror. An ironic note in the setting is the paradoxical reference to the blazing furnaces as Fairy Palaces.

ANALYSIS OF STORY

Hard Times, a social protest novel of nineteenth-century England, is aptly titled. Not only does the working class, known as the "Hands," have a "hard time" in this novel; so do the other classes as well. Dickens divided the novel into three separate books, two of which, "Sowing" and "Reaping," exemplify the Biblical concept of "whatsoever a man soweth, that shall he also reap" (Galatians 6:7).

The third book, entitled "Garnering," Dickens paraphrased from the book of Ruth, in which Ruth garnered grain in the fields of Boaz. Each of his major characters sows, each reaps, and each garners what is left.

A. BOOK ONE: "SOWING"

Book One consists of sixteen chapters in which are sown not only the seeds of the plot but also the seeds of the characters. As these seeds are sown, so shall they be reaped.

Chapters 1, 2, and 3
These chapters, titled "The One Thing Needful," "Murdering the Innocent," and "A Loophole," give the seeds that Thomas Gradgrind sows. He sows the seeds of Fact, not Fancy; of sense, not sentimentality; of conformity, not curiosity. There is only proof, not poetry for him. His very description is one of fact: "square forefinger...square wall of a forehead...square coat...square legs, square shoulders...."

In the second chapter Thomas Gradgrind teaches a lesson as an example for the schoolmaster, Mr. M'Choakumchild, a man who chokes children with Facts. Thomas Gradgrind tries to fill the "little pitchers"—who are numbered, not named—with facts. Sissy Jupe, alone, is the only "little vessel" who cannot be filled with facts, such as the statistical description of a horse. She has lived too long among the "savages" of the circus to perform properly in this school. Here Bitzer, later to show how well he has learned his lesson, can recite all of the physical attributes of a horse.

In the third chapter some of the seeds that Thomas Gradgrind has sown appear not to have taken root. On his way home from his successful lesson to the children, he spies his own children, Louisa and Tom Jr., peeping through a hole at the circus people of Sleary's Horse-riding. Although he had sown seeds of Fact and seeds of not wondering, there was a loophole: his two children desired to learn more than what they had been taught in the "lecturing castle" or in Stone Lodge. At Stone Lodge each of the five little Gradgrinds has his cabinets of Facts which he must absorb. Gradgrind scolds his erring offspring, admonishing them by asking, "What would Mr. Bounderby say?" Here one sees that Gradgrind, though retired from the hardware business and a member of Parliament, is aware of the wealth and influence of the factory owner. The reader sees here, too, that Louisa, a girl of fifteen or sixteen, is protective toward her younger brother, Tom.

Chapter 4 — "Mr. Bounderby"

Chapter 4, "Mr. Bounderby," gives a portrait of this influential man. Described as a "Bully of Humility," he is rich: a banker, merchant, and manufacturer. Although he is forty-seven or forty-eight years of age, he looks older. His one marked physical characteristic is the enlarged vein in his temple. As usual, he is bragging that he is a "self-made man." The reader also meets Mrs. Gradgrind, a pathetic woman who understands little of the world in which she lives. As she listens to Mr. Bounderby's story, the reader can see that he has bored her many times before with his supposedly miserable birth and childhood—born in a ditch, he was abandoned by his mother to the not-so-tender mercies of a drunken grandmother who sold his shoes for liquor and who drank fourteen glasses of intoxicant before breakfast.

When Bounderby is told of Louisa and Tom's grave misdeed of spying on the circus, he accuses Sissy Jupe of corrupting the children of the town and says that she must be removed from the school. Very generously, he forgives Tom and Louisa. As Louisa accepts his kiss, the reader learns that she does not like him. She tells Tom that she would not feel the pain if he were to take a knife and cut out the spot on her cheek that Bounderby had kissed. Jane, the youngest Gradgrind, is pictured asleep, her tear-stained face bent over her slate of fractions.

Chapters 5 and 6

In these two chapters one gets a picture of Coketown and learns that Sissy Jupe's father has abandoned her. Chapter 5, "The Keynote," describes Coketown as a town of red brick sacred to Fact. It is a town in which all of the buildings are so much alike that one cannot distinguish the jail from the infirmary without reading the names of the two inscribed above the doors. It is a town blackened by the "serpent-like" smoke that billows endlessly into the air from the factory chimneys and settles in the lungs of the workers, a town with a black canal and a river that runs purple with industrial waste, a town of eighteen denominations housed in pious warehouses of red brick. Who belongs to these eighteen denominations is the mystery. The laboring classes do not belong, even though there are always petitions to the House of Commons for acts of Parliament to make the laboring classes religious by force. A Teetotal Society has tabular statements showing that people drink; chemists and druggists have tabular statements showing that those who do not drink take opium. Also in this chapter is an analogy between the conformity of the town and the conformity of the Gradgrinds and the other products of Fact.

Bounderby and Gradgrind, on their way to Pod's End, a shabby section of the town, to inform Sissy's father that he must remove her from school before she corrupts the other children, encounter Sissy being chased by Bitzer, the ideal student. They send Bitzer on his way and go with Sissy to see her father. Having gone for "nine oils" for her father's "hurts," Sissy tells the two men about her father's profession as a clown and about Merrylegs, his performing dog. Bounderby, in his usual manner, comments with a metallic laugh, "Merrylegs and nine oils. Pretty well this, for a self-made man."

Chapter 6, entitled "Sleary's Horsemanship," portrays the circus folk, who are in direct contrast to Bounderby and Gradgrind. In this chapter, one learns that Sissy's father, thinking that others will take better care of her than he can, has deserted her. In the Pegasus's Arms, the hotel of the circus people, Bounderby and Gradgrind exchange philosophy with Mr. Sleary, a stout, flabby man, the proprietor of the circus, and with Mr. E. W. B. Childers, and Kidderminster, performers in the circus. The ensuing conversation between the schools of Fact and Fancy reveals that there is little understanding between the two. When Bounderby states that the circus people do not know the value of time and that he has raised himself above such people, Kidderminster replies that Bounderby should lower himself. Sleary's philosophy is that of Dickens, "Make the betht of uth, not the wurtht." (Make the best of it [life], not the worst.)

When Sissy is convinced that her father has deserted her, she accepts Gradgrind's invitation to become a member of his household. Gradgrind's offer is motivated by Fact. Louisa will see what vulgar curiosity will lead to. Sleary encourages Sissy to accept the offer of the "Squire" (the name he has given Gradgrind). He says that she is too old to apprentice; however, he contends that there must be people in the world dedicated to amusing others.

Chapter 7 — "Mrs. Sparsit"
This chapter is one of character portrayal. Here the reader meets Mrs. Sparsit, a member of the ancient Powler stock. A widow left penniless by her spendthrift former husband, she serves as Bounderby's housekeeper. Depicted as a contrast to her employer, she does not contradict Bounderby to his face; however, she despises him for the uncouth person that he is. Here, too, the reader sees being planted the seeds of Bounderby's intentions of marrying

Louisa. He hopes that Sissy will not corrupt Louisa, but that Louisa will be good for Sissy. The chapter concludes with Sissy's being told that she is ignorant and must forget the stories of Fairies and Fancy that she has read to her father.

Chapter 8 — "Never Wonder"

"Never Wonder," the keynote of the Gradgrind educational system, is discussed by Louisa and Tom Gradgrind. Dickens' satire on the educational system is expounded through young Tom's dissatisfaction with his own education and Louisa's desire to do and to learn more. She feels that there is something missing — although she does not know what — or lacking in her life. Tom, calling himself a "donkey," vows to take revenge on his father and the whole educational system. He wishes that he could take gunpowder and blow up the doctrine of Facts. His revenge is that he will enjoy life when he leaves home. He has completed his "cramming" and will soon enter Bounderby's bank. Tom later reveals the secret of his future enjoyment: he tells his sister that, since Bounderby is so fond of her, she can make his life easier by playing up to Bounderby. As they gaze into the fire and "wonder," they are interrupted and scolded for their wondering by their mother, a pathetic woman who does not understand her logical husband. Her complete character can be summarized in one of her own comments: "I really *do* wish that I had never had a family, and then you would have known what it was to do without me!"

Chapter 9 — "Sissy's Progress"

Sissy's education in the Gradgrind home and in M'Choakum-child's school does not progress as rapidly as Mr. Gradgrind would desire. She — reared to wonder, to think, to love, and to believe in Fancy — cannot digest the volumes of Facts and figures given her. She cannot be categorized or catalogued. She cannot learn even the most elementary principles of Practical Economy. Even though Sissy cannot be educated into the ways of the Gradgrinds, she becomes a partial educator of Louisa and young Jane. When she talks with Louisa, she defends her runaway father; in doing so and in repeating some of the stories of the circus, she adds nourishment to the tiny seeds of doubt that have been implanted in Louisa's mind about the training she has received. Daily she inquires of Mr.

Gradgrind if a letter for her has arrived. She does not lose hope of hearing from or about her father. Gradually Sissy teaches Louisa the first lesson of compassion and understanding.

Chapters 10, 11, 12, and 13

Chapters 10, 11, 12, and 13 present a picture of the struggles, the desperation, and the momentary joys of the working class. Entitled "Stephen Blackpool," "No Way Out," "The Old Woman," and "Rachael," they are chapters of character representation, of Dickens' philosophy, and of symbolism.

The tenth chapter injects some of Dickens' philosophy into the character sketch of Stephen Blackpool, a power-loom weaver in the Bounderby mill. Representative of Dickens' picture of the Hands, Stephen, a man of integrity, is forty years of age. Even though he has been married for many years, his wife had left him long ago. In this chapter, the seeds of Stephen's discontent are revealed when he returns to his lonely apartment after walking his beloved Rachael home and finds that his drunken wife has returned. Through the words of Blackpool, the reader learns that Dickens believes the laws of England to be unfair to the poor workingman. On the other hand, Dickens lets Rachael, the woman whom Stephen loves, tell him that he should not be bitter toward the laws. When he realizes that the object of his misery has re-entered his life, he sinks into despair; tied to this disreputable creature, he can never marry Rachael.

The title of the eleventh chapter, "No Way Out," is significant in that it characterizes Stephen's hopeless marriage and the seemingly futile struggles of the working class. This chapter also contains imagery that adds to the tone of the story. Dickens satirizes the Industrial Revolution as he likens the roaring furnace to Fairy Palaces and the factories to elephants from which belch forth the serpents of death-giving smoke. The people must breathe this poison daily as they struggle with the monstrous machines in order to earn a pittance. Dickens also satirizes Malthus' system of determining the economy through arithmetic.

Further, one sees Stephen going to his employer to seek help with his marriage. Bounderby's title could well be "Bully of

Humanity" for the manner in which he deals with this worker. Stephen learns only one thing: the laws are truly for the benefit of the rich. If he leaves his drunken wife or if he harms her or if he marries Rachael or if he just lives with Rachael without the sanction of marriage, Stephen will be punished, for the laws are thus arranged; on the other hand, if he seeks a divorce, he cannot obtain one, for money is the only key that opens the doors of the courts of justice in England. As he leaves Bounderby's house, Stephen concludes that the laws of the land are a muddle. During the entire discussion Mrs. Sparsit listens and seems to agree with her boasting employer. Bounderby terminates the interview with his favorite comment: "I see traces of turtle soup, and venison, and gold spoon in this." In other words, he regards the Hands as people desiring the best of life without working for it.

The twelfth chapter, entitled "The Old Woman," introduces mystery into the novel. As Stephen departs from Bounderby's house, he encounters an old woman who asks eagerly about Bounderby. She seems to be entranced as she looks at Bounderby's house and the factory. Stephen, too dejected concerning his own affairs, answers her many questions but does not wonder as to her interest in his employer.

Again, through satire, Dickens censures the machine age by referring to the towering smoke pipes as Towers of Babel, speaking without being understood. At the end of his long day, Stephen turns his feet homeward, walking slowly, dreading to re-enter the small apartment where his wife lies in a drunken stupor.

In Chapter 13 Dickens enters the story again as he draws a portrait of Rachael, the thirty-five-year-old Hand, as a ministering angel. Through Stephen, Dickens expresses the thought that during the nineteenth century there was no equality among men except at birth and death. Stephen, on entering the apartment, finds his beloved Rachael seated by the bedside of his wife. She tells him that his landlady had summoned her to care for the sick woman. His love for Rachael fills him momentarily as he hears her refer to his wife as one of the sick and the lost, a sister who does not realize what she is doing. He and Rachael sit by the woman's bedside, watching over her while Rachael treats her injuries. As the night lengthens, Stephen falls into a troubled sleep and is wakened just in time to see his wife reach for one of the bottles of antiseptic. The seeds of his misery begin to grow as he watches stupor-like, knowing that if she drinks the poisonous preparation she will die. He seems to be dreaming of his own death, knowing that it would come before he had lived happily. As he watches the woman reach for the instrument of her own death, he sits unmoving. Perhaps the object of his miserable existence will be taken; although frightened at his thoughts, he cannot act as the distraught woman pours from the bottle. But Rachael awakens and seizes the deadly cup. Stephen bows in shame for what he almost let happen, blesses Rachael as an angel, and tells her that her act has saved him from complete destruction. She consoles him and leaves the apartment, knowing that he will not weaken again. To him she is the shining star that illuminates the night as compared to the heavy candle that dispels only a little of the darkness that shrouds the world.

Chapters 14, 15, and 16

These three chapters, "The Great Manufacturer," "Father and Daughter," and "Husband and Wife," complete the sowing of seeds for the major characters.

The first, "The Great Manufacturer," is a time-span chapter. Several years have passed since the previous one; Tom has gone to work in Bounderby's bank; Louisa has become a woman; Sissy has been adjudged hopeless as to her progress in education, but accepted because of her kindness and goodness. In the concluding pages of the chapter the seeds of marriage are sown. Here one sees, too, that young Tom's seeds of revenge are growing to maturity. Away from his father's house, he has learned and has come to like the ways of the world. He uses Louisa's love for him to encourage her to accept the proposal that he knows is forthcoming from Bounderby. The seeds of wonder are growing in Louisa; yet they have not been nourished enough to deter her from accepting only facts.

In the next chapter, "Father and Daughter," Mr. Gradgrind presents Bounderby's proposal of marriage to Louisa. When he does, Louisa asks him if he thinks that she loves Bounderby. His embarrassed answer is one that brings a second question to her lips. "What would you advise me to use in its stead?" (instead of love.) His answer is in keeping with his philosophy: "to consider the question simply as one of tangible Fact." Louisa accepts the proposal by stating that there is no other answer for her; she has had no experience of the heart to guide her; she has never been allowed to wonder or to question. The only one who shows any emotional reaction to Gradgrind's announcement of his daughter's betrothal to Bounderby is Sissy, who regards Louisa with pity mingled with wonder and sorrow.

In the final chapter of Book One Bounderby and Louisa are married. When Bounderby imparts to Mrs. Sparsit the news of his coming marriage, she wishes him happiness, but with condescension and compassion. She feels a pity for this aging man who is foolish enough to believe that a woman as young as Louisa can make him a satisfactory wife. When he announces to Mrs. Sparsit the forthcoming nuptials, Bounderby makes plans for her welfare. He offers her an apartment over the bank and her regular stipend for being a keeper of the bank. Mrs. Sparsit realizes that he is doing this only because of her former position with him. Being deposed from her position does not agree with the lady; nevertheless, she accepted the offer rather than eat the bread of dependency.

The courtship was not one of love but one of facts. Dresses were made, jewelry was ordered, all preparations went forward. A church wedding, naturally in the New Church, the only one of the eighteen that differed slightly in architecture, took place. Only once during the entire proceedings did Louisa lose her composure: that was upon parting from her brother, Tom, who was an inadequate support for the occasion. Her brother, whose whole concern in the matter was his own welfare, made light of her fears and sent her to the waiting Bounderby.

B. BOOK TWO – "REAPING"

Consisting of twelve chapters, the second book depicts the harvest – meager for some, abundant for others. Mr. Bounderby, having sowed seeds of unkindness, reaped an unhappy marriage and the loss of his wife; Mr. Gradgrind's seeds of logic and Fact led to disillusionment and destruction; Louisa Gradgrind Bounderby, sowed with the seeds of Fact, reaped unhappiness; for Tom, the seeds of dishonesty produced a harvest of loneliness and destruction; Stephen planted seeds of discontent and reaped ostracism by his kind. Each character reaped a harvest of his own making.

Chapter 1 — "Effects in the Bank"
Apparent immediately is Dickens' satire, setting the tone for this chapter and the entire book. It begins, "A sunny midsummer day. There was such a thing sometimes, even in Coketown." Even in Coketown, the rays of sunlight, or reforms, penetrated the smoke and the fog—mistreatment of the workers and the duping of the factory owners. Even in Coketown there had come a time when the laboring class united for self-preservation and education for their children. Not only the workers but also the entire town "seemed to be frying in oil": Bounderby, in the oil of Mrs. Sparsit's pity; young Tom, in the oil of her suspicions; Bitzer, in the oil of her disdain; Louisa, in the oil of destruction. Guardians of the bank by night and spies by the day, Mrs. Sparsit and Bitzer were ill-matched companions; nevertheless, they were bound together by Fact. Bitzer, grown from the brilliant student of Fact into a cold young man of self-interest, shared not only tasks in the bank with Mrs. Sparsit but also the desire to undermine the position of young Tom. In this chapter the reader learns that Mr. Gradgrind has reared a son who is an idler and a parasite.

Introduced in this chapter is another character who is going to be influential in helping Louisa reap unhappiness and in helping Bounderby gather the just harvest of his pretensions. By mistake he meets Mrs. Sparsit first and inquires about Louisa; Mrs. Sparsit's replies pique his interest.

Chapter 2 — "Mr. James Harthouse"
Introduced in Chapter 2 by name is the stranger of Chapter 1. James (Jem) Harthouse, a young man bored with all of his travels and education, comes to work in the service of Gradgrind's political party. Upon first meeting Bounderby, Harthouse is unimpressed by

the "self-made man" story or by the pride of Bounderby—the smoke that is the "meat and drink" of Coketown. Here Dickens subtly lets the reader know that this "meat and drink" to Bounderby is the death and destruction of the workers.

Bounderby takes Mr. Harthouse home for dinner in order to meet Louisa. Harthouse is singularly struck by the bareness of the room that he enters, which, devoid of a woman's touch, is a symbol of the sterility of the life that exists there. Intrigued by Louisa's detachment and the withdrawn expression of her eyes, Harthouse decides that his next challenge is to arouse some response in those eyes. When introduced to Tom—whom he immediately nicknames the "whelp" because of the younger man's manners and attitude—Harthouse sees the first flicker of emotion in Louisa's face and realizes that she lavishes upon her brother all of the love of which she is capable. Carefully, by encouraging Tom's friendship, Harthouse plants the seeds that will win Louisa's confidence.

Chapter 3—"The Whelp"
The seeds of Facts planted by Thomas Gradgrind in his son have become a harvest of deceit and hypocrisy. Flattered by Harthouse's interest, Tom reveals the circumstances of Louisa's marriage to Bounderby. Bragging that he was the only one who could influence her, Tom, while he drinks Harthouse's liquor and smokes his cigars, discusses Louisa's having never loved. Harthouse leads Tom on until he learns all that he wishes to know about Bounderby, Mrs. Sparsit, and Louisa. More and more Harthouse becomes enchanted by the prospect of the "chase." Dickens concludes the chapter by philosophizing that Tom is so ignorant that he does not realize the damage he has done.

Chapters 4, 5, and 6
The next three chapters, entitled "Men and Brothers," "Men and Masters," and "Fading Away," focus upon Stephen and his relationship with his fellow workers, his encounter with his employer, and his loss of employment.

In Chapter 4, Dickens pictures the workers seeking to lessen the burdens of their lives. The labor-union agitator, Slackbridge, is the supposed "saviour" for the workers as they make their voices of protest heard. Dickens shows that the labor leaders may be as corrupt as the employers; he depicts the laboring class grasping at straws and led by a Judas or a false prophet. Of the laboring group, Stephen is the only one who cannot agree with Slackbridge's ideas; consequently, Slackbridge uses him as an example and turns the other workers against Stephen. When Stephen announces his decision not to join the union, the workers are convinced that "private feeling must yield to the common cause." Ostracized by his fellow workers, Stephen walks alone, afraid even to see his beloved Rachael. At the conclusion of the chapter Bitzer comes to him and tells him that Bounderby wishes to see him.

In "Men and Masters" Stephen defends the workers against Bounderby, who calls them the "pests of the earth." Stephen says that he has not refused to join the union because of his loyalty to Bounderby but because he has made a promise. Although his own fellow workers distrust him, he is faithful to them and gives his reasons for needed reform, thus infuriating Bounderby, who dismisses him from his job in the factory. Dickens' philosophy is expressed in the conversation as Stephen tells Bounderby that men are not machines, that they do have souls. After Bounderby, who cannot bear to hear any truth except his own, fires him, Stephen leaves the large "brick castle" saying, "Heaven help us in this world." The discussion between Bounderby and Stephen has made a deep impression upon Louisa.

In the sixth chapter, "Fading Away," many threads of the plot appear. Upon leaving Bounderby's house, Stephen meets Rachael and the old woman whom he had met some time before standing outside Bounderby's house. The old woman questions Stephen carefully about Bounderby's wife. When she hears that Louisa is young and handsome, she seems delighted. Again, Stephen wonders little about the woman's curiosity concerning Bounderby. He tells Rachael he has been fired and that he plans to leave Coketown to seek employment elsewhere. He tries to make her understand that it would be better for her if she were not seen with him anymore. Later at his room, where he and Rachael are talking with the old woman, who calls herself Mrs. Pegler, Louisa and her brother Tom come to see Stephen. For the first time Louisa has come to the home of one of the workers. She knows well the facts of supply and demand, the percentage of pauperism and the percentage of crime, and the results of the changes in wheat prices; but she knows nothing of the workers who make up these statistics. Indeed, to her they have been just so many units producing a given amount of goods in a given amount of time and space. For the first time she realizes that these people are not mere statistics; they have pride; they struggle to exist. She learns, too, that if a worker is fired from his job, he will not be able to find another one in the same town.

As she talks with Stephen and Rachael, she feels compassion for them and offers Stephen money to help him find employment away from Coketown. When Stephen accepts two pounds from her, Louisa is impressed with his self-command.

Tom remains quiet while Louisa converses with Rachael and Stephen. When he sees his sister ready to depart, he asks Stephen to step out on the stairs with him while Louisa remains inside the room talking with Rachael. Tom persuades Stephen that he may be able to do something for the discharged worker during the few days remaining before his departure from Coketown in search of work. Tom hints strongly about a job as a light porter at the bank. Stephen wonders about, but does not question, the strange request made of him to wait outside the bank for a while each evening. Stephen agrees to grant the request. During his three days of fruitless waiting, Stephen is probably observed by Mrs. Sparsit and Bitzer. At the end of that period, having completed the work on his loom, Stephen takes leave of Rachael and departs from Coketown.

Dickens weaves into this chapter some third-person narration concerning the fate of the workers. He says, "Utilitarian economists, skeletons of schoolmasters, Commissioners of Fact, genteel and used-up infidels, gabblers of many little dog's-eared creeds, the poor you will have always with you." He urges these people to give the poor some consideration, lest they — when nothing is left except a bare existence — rise up and destroy their oppressors.

Chapter 7 – "Gunpowder"

Aptly named "Gunpowder," this chapter shows that three characters – Louisa, Tom, and Jem Harthouse – are figuratively sitting on kegs of explosives.

Harthouse, having performed his duties well, has gained the confidence of both Gradgrind and Bounderby. They are unaware of his objective: to make Louisa love him. His pursuit of Louisa is amusing to him, and he becomes a frequent caller at the Bounderby house. The reader learns that Bounderby, having foreclosed a mortgage on Nickits, who speculated too much, has moved his family into a country estate some fifteen miles from Coketown and accessible by railway. In the flower garden Bounderby has planted cabbages; in the house filled with elegant furnishings and beautiful paintings, Boundery has continued his barrack-like existence.

The day of Harthouse's triumph arrives at Bounderby's country home, when he broaches to Louisa the subject of Tom's gambling by saying he is interested in Tom's well-being. He convinces Louisa of his deep interest in Tom. While they are walking back to the house, they encounter Tom carving a girl's name in a tree. Tom, in a bad mood, is barely civil to his sister, who has refused him a hundred pounds. When Louisa goes into the house, Harthouse remains in the garden with Tom. Persuaded by Harthouse, Tom discusses his troubles with him. When Harthouse asks Tom how much money he needs, Tom replies by saying it is too late for money. Harthouse persuades Tom to apologize to Louisa for his rudeness. When Tom does apologize, Louisa believes that the change in him is due to Harthouse's influence; her smile is for Harthouse now.

Chapter 8 – "Explosion"

When gunpowder is set off, an explosion always follows. Accordingly, this chapter is well named. It has a twofold purpose: to relate the bank robbery and to show Louisa's growing fondness for Harthouse and her continued awakening to the realization that something is missing from her life.

The chapter opens with Harthouse smoking his pipe and musing over the happenings of the preceding night. Pleased with

himself at the turn of events, he did not dwell long on the conse-
quences of what could happen as a result of his relationship with
Louisa. Here the reader sees Dickens drawing an analogy between
Harthouse and the Devil. Harthouse departs early for a public
occasion, at some distance from the Bounderby residence. When he
returns to the Bounderby house at six, he is met by Bounderby, who
informs him of the robbery at the bank. Whoever entered the bank
did so with a false key; the key was later found in the street. One
hundred and fifty pounds is the missing sum. At the Bounderby
house are Bitzer, who is scolded for sleeping so soundly, and Mrs.
Sparsit, who has come to stay because her nerves are too bad for
her to remain in her apartment at the bank. Bounderby comments
that even Louisa fainted when she learned of the robbery. The
reader realizes almost immediately the identity of the thief, but
Stephen Blackpool is suspected of the crime. Coming under suspicion
as an accomplice is the old woman who is yet a mystery to all.
When Harthouse inquires concerning Tom's whereabouts, Bounderby says he is helping the police.

As the evening progresses, Mrs. Sparsit obliges her employer
by occasionally resorting to copious tears as she caters to Bounderby's whims—playing backgammon with him and preparing his
sherry with lemon-peel and nutmeg—and watches Louisa and Harthouse, hoping for the worst.

Louisa lies sleepless waiting for Tom's return; she is concerned, for she suspects that he—not Blackpool—has forced open
the safe and used the false key, if indeed it were used. An hour past
midnight she hears Tom enter. After giving him time to prepare for
bed, she goes to his upstairs room, hoping that he will confide in her.
They discuss their visit with Blackpool and Rachael and agree not
to tell anyone about it. Tom lies to Louisa, telling her that he had
taken Stephen outside on the stairs that night to tell him what good
fortune he had in getting her help. Troubled, Louisa leaves her
brother, who weeps, unable to confide in her or anyone else.

Chapter 9—"Hearing the Last of It"
    "Hearing the Last of It" bears a dual meaning: the last of
Louisa's determination to remain aloof from Harthouse and the last

of Mrs. Sparsit's scheme to be again the respected housekeeper in the Bounderby house. This dual meaning is incomplete until the final chapter of this book.

In spite of her "bad nerves," Mrs. Sparsit reassumes all of her duties as housekeeper and hostess in Bounderby's house. Even though she refers to Louisa as Miss Gradgrind, Bounderby takes no offense. He is pathetic in his acceptance of the old regime—his tea poured, a ready ear, a smooth-running household, and an obvious, agreeable admirer of his talents as a "self-made man."

The reader realizes that Mrs. Sparsit is aware of the dangerous alienation of husband and wife. She kisses Bounderby's hand when she is in his presence, but shakes her right-hand mitten at his picture in his absence and says, "Serve you right, you Noodle, and I am glad of it." Mrs. Sparsit's constant reference to Louisa as Miss Gradgrind lets the reader know also that no real marriage exists between the aging tyrant and the young woman just awakening to life.

Louisa is summoned home to see her gravely ill mother. Since her marriage, she has been home very few times. Now as she returns, she has no childhood memories to make her homecoming glad. Rather she goes with a heavy, hardened kind of sorrow to find her mother rapidly sinking. In those last minutes of Mrs. Gradgrind's life, Louisa lets the reader know how much Sissy has influenced her and the youngest Gradgrind child, Jane.

Chapters 10, 11, and 12

The final three chapters of this book are chapters of complete harvest: unhappiness for Louisa and the destruction of Gradgrind's philosophy and of Bounderby's pride.

Chapter 10, entitled "Mrs. Sparsit's Staircase," is one of symbolism. Not only is the "staircase" a staircase erected in Mrs. Sparsit's mind as symbolic of Louisa's eventual shame for the dark at the bottom, but it is also the staircase of destruction for many of the other characters.

After several weeks at the Bounderby home, Mrs. Sparsit returns to her apartment at the bank. On the eve of her departure,

Mr. Bounderby invites her to be a constant weekend guest at his home. Following this invitation, she and Mr. Bounderby discuss the bank robbery. Bounderby says that Rome was not built in a day and neither will the thief be discovered in such a short period of time. He adds that if Romulus and Remus could wait, so can he; for he and they have much in common: they had had a she-wolf for a nurse; he, a she-wolf for a grandmother. He makes reference not only to Tom's diligence at the bank but also to the old woman, who is under suspicion.

Constant companions, Louisa and Harthouse discuss the robbery. Louisa cannot believe that Stephen could rob the bank. Meanwhile Mrs. Sparsit watches the growing friendship between the two and does nothing to prevent the disaster she knows will come.

"Lower and Lower," the next chapter, depicts Mrs. Sparsit's watchful waiting for Louisa's complete descent into the black gulf at the bottom of the staircase. It also shows Gradgrind's unemotional acceptance of his wife's death; he hurries home, buries her in a business-like manner, and returns to his "dust-throwing" in Parliament.

Even though Mrs. Sparsit is not at the Bounderby country residence during the week, she manages to keep a close watch on Louisa through talk with Bounderby, Tom, and Harthouse. When Mrs. Sparsit learns that Bounderby is to be away for three or four days on business, she, inviting Tom to dinner, skillfully worms from him information concerning Louisa and Harthouse. When she learns that Harthouse is expected back the next afternoon from a hunting trip to Yorkshire and that he has asked Tom to meet him, Mrs. Sparsit gloats over Louisa's final descent. She first suspects, then learns, that Harthouse is using the ruse of Tom's meeting him to be alone with Louisa.

The next afternoon she goes out to the Bounderby country residence and looks for the pair. Hiding behind a tree in the woods, she hears Harthouse, who has returned by horseback, declare his love for Louisa and urge her to go away with him. A storm rises and the rain begins to fall in sheets. Afraid of discovery, Mrs. Sparsit is drenched as she watches Louisa leave Harthouse and go into the house. Much to her delight, Mrs. Sparsit sees Louisa, clothed in a cloak and hat, leave the house and go to the railroad station. Following her, Mrs. Sparsit—drenched, cold and sneezing—bursts into tears when, after the train arrives in Coketown, she realizes that she has lost Louisa.

The final chapter of this book, entitled "Down," is significant in that the reader sees Mr. Gradgrind's philosophy crumbling around him as his daughter, Louisa, falls in an insensible heap at his feet.

When the chapter opens the reader sees Mr. Gradgrind, home from Parliament, occupied in his usual pursuit—working with statistics, unmindful of the pouring rain and storm. He is startled as the door opens and Louisa enters. Fleeing to the house of her birth for refuge against the emotions which stir her and which she does not understand, she curses the day of her birth, challenges her father's philosophy to save her now, and explains to him why she married Bounderby. Although she tells her father of Harthouse's declaration of love and his desire that they elope, she assures him that she has not disgraced the family name. As he sees the crumbling of his dogma, he reacts as a father who loves his daughter. He holds her in his arms, not knowing how to comfort her. The book ends with her, the symbol of all his teachings, lying in an insensible heap at his feet.

C. BOOK THREE — "GARNERING"

Just as the Biblical Ruth garnered in the fields of Boaz picking up the wheat dropped by the reapers, so do the characters garner or pick up what the grim reapers of experience have left behind. Thomas Gradgrind, after realizing the failure of his system, tries to help his children to pick up the pieces of his and their shattered lives. Returning to bachelorhood, Bounderby, exposed as a fraud, garners a life of loneliness, dying perhaps in the streets of Coketown. As they sowed, as they reaped, so must they reassemble what is left.

Chapters 1, 2, and 3
The first three chapters—"Another Thing Needful," "Very Ridiculous," and "Very Decided"—primarily concern Louisa's

fight for self-understanding. Here Thomas Gradgrind reverses the thing needed; he bears out Dickens' beliefs that people's emotions cannot be measured in statistics. In the first chapter of the novel the thing needed was a factual education, a concern of the head; in the first chapter of the final book of the novel, the thing needed is understanding and compassion, a concern of the heart. In this chapter, too, the reader learns that Jane Gradgrind, the younger daughter, is leading and will continue to lead a life quite different from that which her older sister has led. Facts mixed with Fancy, statistics mixed with compassion, love, and understanding will shape her life. Under the influence of Sissy, she will grow into another Sissy, but a better educated Sissy.

Even though Gradgrind blames himself for the unhappiness that has come to Louisa, she does not blame him. Rather, in the conclusion of the chapter, she—bewildered and lost with no consolation from her education of Facts—turns to Sissy, begging for help.

In the second chapter, the reader finds Sissy—modest, shy, gentle Sissy—taking into her own hands matters concerning Louisa. This chapter also depicts the ridiculous situation in which Harthouse finds himself. Harthouse, who spends an anxious and uneasy twenty-four hours after Louisa leaves him, is taken aback at the appearance of Sissy at his quarters. Although he argues with her, he bows to her command that he leave Coketown, never to see Louisa again. Had any person other than the innocent Sissy gone to him, he might have reacted differently.

After Sissy takes her leave of him, he writes three letters: one to his brother declaring his boredom with Coketown, one to Bounderby announcing his departure, and one to Gradgrind stating that he is leaving his position. Calling himself the "Great Pyramid of Failure," he proves himself to be a very shallow and selfish man: he is concerned only with what the "fellows" will think if they learn of his failure.

"Very Decided," the title of the third chapter, could describe Bounderby, Thomas Gradgrind, and Louisa.

Having lost Louisa in the dark and rain and being anxious to bear the tidings to Bounderby, Mrs. Sparsit goes to London and seeks him out at his hotel in St. James' Street. Although she has a sore throat from her drenching and is barely able to talk, Mrs. Sparsit relates the news of Louisa's supposed elopement and faints at the feet of the great "self-made man." Later she and Bounderby rush back to Coketown to inform Gradgrind of his daughter's disgrace. When Bounderby learns that Louisa is at Stone Lodge and that her father proposes to keep her for awhile, he becomes furious. He delivers his ultimatum: if Louisa has not returned to his house by noon the next day, he will send her clothing and conclude that she prefers to stay with her family. Should she decide not to return, he will no longer be responsible for her.

The reader learns from the conversation and manner of the two men that Gradgrind has undergone some change of philosophy. Bounderby becomes infuriated, probably because Gradgrind uses words almost identical to those spoken by Bounderby to Stephen in discussing Stephen's responsibilities toward his wife. He reacts in a manner in keeping with Josiah Bounderby, the "self-made man" of Coketown. According to Bounderby, the incompatibility is that of Loo Bounderby, who might have been better left Loo Gradgrind. True to his expected pattern, he comments that she wants "turtle soup and venison, with a gold spoon."

When Louisa does not return to Bounderby's house the next day, he sends her clothing and personal belongings to her, begins negotiations to sell the country house, returns to his town house in Coketown, and reassumes his life as a bachelor.

Chapters 4 and 5 — "Lost" and "Found"

The titles of these two chapters show the loss and the finding of many things: Bounderby's loss of his "miserable childhood" and the town's finding he has a mother; Louisa's loss of a husband and a belief in Facts and the finding of a loving friend and an understanding of others; and Gradgrind's loss of faith in his system and a finding of love and understanding for his family.

Bounderby does not let his broken marriage interfere with his business; indeed, he pursues the bank robbery with more vigor,

40

offering twenty pounds for Stephen's apprehension. The boldly
painted reward poster is read by those who can read and to those
who cannot. Each person has his own ideas concerning the inno-
cence or guilt of Stephen. To strengthen his position with the workers, Slackbridge capitalizes upon Stephen's "disgrace."

Bounderby brings Rachael and Tom to Louisa to confirm or to
deny Rachael's story of Louisa and Tom's visit to Stephen's home
that evening so long ago. Rachael, though she would rather not, believes that Louisa has had something to do with Stephen's being
accused of the robbery. Tom is upset when Louisa admits their
visit to Stephen's room and her offer of financial aid to Stephen.

When Rachael admits under questioning that she has had a
letter from Stephen, who has taken an assumed name in order to
obtain a job, Bounderby is positive that Stephen has done this in
order to prevent discovery of the robbery. Rachael sends Stephen a
letter asking him to return to Coketown to clear his name. When
Stephen does not come at the end of the fourth day, Rachael tells
Bounderby under what name and in which town Stephen is working.
Messengers sent to bring Stephen back cannot find him. As the
days pass, the people of the town are divided in their attitudes and
beliefs concerning him and the robbery.

"Found," the title of Chapter 5, is symbolic of the events.
Days pass; life goes on; Rachael finds a friend, Sissy, who shares
her heartbreak and anxiety. Found is Bounderby's mother. The
mysterious Mrs. Pegler, taken against her will before Bounderby
by Mrs. Sparsit, refutes his story of a miserable childhood after
Gradgrind scolds Mrs. Pegler for being an unnatural mother. Cutting a ridiculous figure, the "Bully of Humility" refuses to comment
on Mrs. Pegler's story of his secure childhood, of his forsaking her,
and of his pensioning her off on thirty pounds a year providing she
would stay away from him.

Chapter 6 — "The Starlight"
In her grief over Stephen's not returning, Rachael turns to Sissy
for comfort and companionship. On a Sunday morning more than a
week after Stephen's disappearance, she and Sissy are walking in

the fields near Coketown. They find Stephen's hat and discover he had fallen into Old Hell Shaft, an abandoned mine shaft. When they summon help, the local villagers mobilize, rig up a windlass and bucket, and rescue him. His body broken and wasted from starvation, Stephen is hoisted from the shaft. He lives long enough to request that Gradgrind clear his name of robbery, thus implicating Tom, Gradgrind's son; to ask Louisa's forgiveness for believing that she had plotted to harm him; and to say that all men should learn to live together with understanding. Stephen dies quietly, his hand in Rachael's and his eyes gazing at the star that had been his source of comfort in his prison. The march back to Coketown is a funeral procession.

Chapter 7 — "Whelp-Hunting"

When Gradgrind realizes that his son is a thief, he retires to his room for twenty-four hours, not coming out even to eat or drink. Upon deciding to help his son, he learns from Sissy that she has sent him to Sleary's circus for refuge. The three journey separately to the circus—Gradgrind alone and Sissy and Louisa together. There they find Tom masquerading as a black-face comic. The ensuing conversation between Gradgrind and Sleary indicates that Gradgrind's system of education, shaped by the economic conditions of the time, has been destroyed. From Sleary they learn what has happened to the circus people and with him they plan Tom's escape. Tom is surly with his father and Louisa, heaping coals on the fire of Gradgrind's grief by referring to Facts—statistics which show that a certain percentage of people employed in positions of trust are dishonest. Gradgrind plans to send Tom to Liverpool and then abroad; however, Bitzer suddenly appears and interferes.

Chapters 8 and 9

Chapters 8 and 9 conclude the final book of the novel; entitled "Philosophical" and "Final," they complete Gradgrind's realization of the complete destruction of his system of education and serve as Dickens' prophecies of what is to come. When Bitzer stops Tom's escape, Gradgrind asks Bitzer if he has a heart. Bitzer replies, "The circulation, sir, couldn't be carried on without one. No man, sir, acquainted with the facts established by Harvey relating to the circulation of the blood can doubt that I have a heart." When Gradgrind, by asking him how much money he wants, tries to persuade

Bitzer not to return Tom to Bounderby, Bitzer reveals that his sole purpose is to gain a promotion to Tom's former job. In the course of the conversation Bitzer says that "...the whole social system is a question of self-interest." The reader learns here that Dickens believed the economic system of nineteenth-century England was based on self-interest. Though in front of Bitzer Mr. Sleary feigns indignation that Gradgrind wants him to help Tom — Gradgrind's thieving son — escape, he makes use of a dancing horse and a trained dog to harass Bitzer while Mr. Childers drives Tom to safety.

Sleary, telling Gradgrind that Signor Jupe's dog Merrylegs has returned to the circus, says that Jupe is surely dead. The circus people had agreed not to reveal Jupe's death to Sissy, his daughter. It seems a bit ironic that Sleary is the one to refute Bitzer's statement that the whole social system is based on self-interest, for the circus people and their understanding have shown that there is also love.

A sadder and wiser Gradgrind takes his leave of the circus people with Sleary's words ringing in his ears: "People mutht be amuthed. They can't be alwayth a-learning, nor yet they can't be alwayth a-working, they an't made for it. You *mutht* have uth, Thquire. Do the withe thing and the kind thing too, and make the betht of uth, not the wurtht!"

It seems significant, too, that the novel opens with the children in class and closes with them at a circus.

In "Final" the future is anticipated by Dickens. He foretells Mrs. Sparsit's lot with her complaining relative, Lady Scadgers, Mr. Bounderby's death in the streets of his smoke-filled town, Bitzer's rise in position, Sissy's happy marriage blessed with children, Gradgrind's being scorned by his former associates for his learning Hope, Faith, and Charity, and Tom's penitence and death thousands of miles away. Dickens also pictures Louisa — loved by Sissy's children and the children of others, but none of her own — seeking to understand and to help others. With hope for a brighter future for the children and the working classes of England, Dickens concludes his novel.

DICKENS' PHILOSOPHY AND STYLE

Charles Dickens, required to write *Hard Times* in twenty
sections to be published over a period of five months, filled the novel
with his own philosophy and symbolism. Dickens expounds his
philosophy in two ways: through straight third-person exposition
and through the voices of his characters. His approach to reality is
allegorical in nature; his plot traces the effect of rational education
on Gradgrind's two children. He presents two problems in the text
of his novel; the most important one is that of the educational
system and what divides the school of Facts and the circus school of
Fancy. The conflicts of the two worlds of the schoolroom and the
circus represent the adult attitudes toward life. While the schoolroom dehumanizes the little scholars, the circus, all fancy and love,
restores humanity. The second problem deals with the economic
relationships of labor and management. Here one sees that Dickens
lets the educational system be dominated by, rather than serve, the
economic system. His philosophy, expounded through his characters, is best summarized by Sleary, who says that men should
make the best of life, not the worst of it.

His symbolism takes such forms as Coketown's being a brick
jungle, strangled in sameness and smoke, the belching factories as
elephants in this jungle, the smoke as treacherous snakes, and the
children as little "vessels" which must be filled. His symbolism also
becomes allegorical as he utilizes Biblical connotation in presenting
the moral structure of the town and the people.

In addition to dialogue, straight narration, and description,
Dickens employs understatement to convey through satire the
social, economic, and educational problems and to propose solu-
tions for these problems. His often tongue-in-cheek statements
balance the horror of the scenery by the absurdity of humor, based
on both character and theme.

STUDY QUESTIONS

1. Critics have called *Hard Times* an allegory. Would you
agree with this statement? Prove your response by making
direct reference to passages in the novel.

2. Characterize Mrs. Gradgrind; in what ways does she show that, being incapable of comprehending her husband's philosophy, she has withdrawn from the world?

3. Louisa was descending the allegorical staircase of shame. Were there others descending with her? Support your answer.

4. What analogy is drawn between Coketown and the Gradgrindian philosophy?

5. What are Mrs. Sparsit's reasons for not calling Louisa Mrs. Bounderby?

6. Explain what Dickens means by "Bounderby's absolute power."

7. Rachael and Stephen have been subjected to criticism by readers who say that they are almost too good to be true. At what points in the story do Rachael and Stephen refute this criticism?

8. What is Mrs. Sparsit's role in the novel?

9. Dickens, as we all know, is utilizing satire to agitate for better conditions in England. To what advantage does Kidderminster serve Dickens' purpose?

10. What motivated Louisa's visit to Stephen? What were the results of this visit?

11. What, according to Tom, was Louisa's method of escape?

12. Of what significance was the "Star Shining" to Stephen? What does this represent symbolically?

13. In the time of the Hebrew prophet Daniel, Belshazzar, last king of Babylon, saw the "handwriting on the wall," which foretold his destruction. How does Dickens utilize this analogy?

14. Why is it significant for the novel to open in the classroom of Facts and conclude in the circus of Fancy?

15. What hope does Dickens give concerning Gradgrind?

16. By clearing Stephen's name, Mr. Gradgrind realized that someone else would be implicated. Who was this person? How does Gradgrind react when he realizes the implications?

17. How does Bounderby's concept of smoke differ from that of the Hands?

18. What is the motive behind Mrs. Sparsit's spying on James Harthouse and Louisa Bounderby?

19. Bitzer states that the entire economic system is based on self-interest. Does his character prove his statement? What characters other than Bitzer would be examples of his statement?

20. How did Gradgrind react when he realized that his educational philosophy was a failure?

NOTES

NOTES

NOTES

(for comparing @ Mayor of Casterbridge)

I. WRITING STYLE
   A. Clearly Victorian

   B. Wordings

II. CHARACTER PROTRAYAL
   A. Both Hardy and Dickens takes representative
   from both classes in English society
   (rich & poor)
   B. There is not always a definite antagonist
   + protagonist but instead they are both
   constantly changing.